Contents

Some words are printed in bold, **like this**. You can find out what they mean by looking in the glossary on page 30.

Introduction

So far, Will Smith's life story has been a list of successes. He always puts masses of energy into anything he does. He once said, "When I was young I realised that the person that works the hardest wins." He is known as a perfectionist, which means he wants to do everything perfectly. He aims to do the best he can, and to try to win people's admiration.

Multi-talented

Will Smith is unusual because he has been able to cross over from one art form to another, and to another, with ease. He has been a successful pop singer, television actor, movie actor, and **producer**. Few people are skilled actors and singers, and fewer still are successful in both.

Will Smith ran two careers side by side. While a movie star, he was a singer, too.

Will's latest success is in becoming a movie producer. Here he is on the set of *Hancock*, a movie he produced in 2007–08.

Sometimes, he has kept more than one job going at a time. In 1997 he had a leading role in the movie *Men in Black*. He sang the main song for the movie, too.

Charming

This extraordinary performer has the ability to make people feel at ease. His friendliness, humour, and charm have brought him famous friends, such as Tom Cruise. People like to work with him because they know he will always do his best. His supportive fans are all ages and races.

Leading the way

Will Smith is one of the few African-Americans to get a lead role in a series of blockbuster movies. He is an **inspiration** to many African-American actors because, in the United States, white actors are more usually offered the star parts in films.

Early influences

Will's full name is Willard Christopher Smith Jr. (Junior). He was born on 25 September 1968, in the city of Philadelphia, Pennsylvania, USA. There was nothing very special about the neighbourhood where he was born. The area was called Winfield. The people who lived there were neither rich nor poor.

Will's family

Will's father, Willard Smith Sr. (Senior), owned a company that sold freezers to supermarkets. Will's mother, Caroline, worked for the local school. Will was the second eldest child of four. He had an older sister, Pamela, and a younger brother and sister who were twins. Their names were Ellen and Harry.

Will was born in the suburbs of the city of Philadelphia, USA.

"The Prince"

At school, Will was always at the centre of things. He was always asking questions and cracking a joke. His charm often got him out of trouble. Teachers forgave him if he forgot his homework or was late because he was so polite and funny.

Will's friends and teachers began to call him "Prince Charming". This was shortened to "The Prince". Will later added "Fresh" to his nickname – he called himself the "Fresh Prince".

Worries

Will was not always sure of himself. He worried that his ears stuck out too much. "One guy once told me that I looked like a car with the doors open", he said. He used his jokes to stop bullies focusing on him.

This is Overbrook High School, where Will charmed his teachers.

A strict father

Will's parents were quite strict. His father used to be in the Air Force. He showed Will the self-discipline (how to control behaviour and work hard) he had learnt. As a boy, Will did not like his father being so strict but self-discipline became a useful tool on his road to success. Will said, "I was so petrified of my parents that I managed to avoid most of the pitfalls that teens fall in."

Will Smith with his father, Will Smith Sr. Will's father taught him some useful lessons while he was a boy.

You can do anything

Will's father taught him that he could do anything if he really wanted to. One day, Will Sr. told Will and his brother to rebuild the brick wall in front of his business. Will and his brother did not think they could mix so much cement and lay so many bricks. After they had finished, Will's father said, "Don't you ever tell me there's something you can't do."

Will often saw his father fitting freezers in supermarket basements, amongst rats and mud. It was a lesson for Will. Will wanted to make sure he never had to work amongst rats and mud.

Teenage temptations

Crime and drugs were common in parts of Philadelphia. Will's father worried that these things might tempt his teenage son. To keep him away from it all, he drove Will round the poorer parts of Philadelphia. Seeing homeless people and drug addicts was a warning to Will – to stay away from crime and drugs.

Will's father drove him around the poorer parts of the city. Will saw the misery caused by drugs and poverty.

Fresh Prince

When Will was still at school, a new style of music was becoming popular in the United States. It was called **hip-hop** music. A few years later, it would be a major part of his life.

Rap

Hip-hop music began with **rap** in the 1970s, in New York, USA. Rap is a bit like poetry but it always **rhymes** and always has a strong, fast **rhythm**. The words are often about the rapper's life. They also give the rapper's opinions on different topics. While rapping, a drumbeat is often played in the background.

The Sugarhill Gang made the first successful rap/hip-hop record.

In the 1970s **DJs** took the beats from other music, such as rock songs. While playing the recorded beat, they or others rapped. In the United States, rap suddenly became popular with young people who were fed up with **disco music**. It was especially popular with African-Americans who lived in New York.

The first rap **single** was "Rapper's Delight" (1979) by The Sugarhill Gang. Will heard the song on the radio when he was 11 years old. Straightaway, he started rapping, too.

A musician in Grandmaster Flash and the Furious Five was the first to use the term "hip-hop".

Hip-hop music

By the 1980s rap had reached other countries, including the UK. Rap also became known as hip-hop music. Hip-hop is now a culture (way of life) for many young people. It has its own music, fashion, and art.

In the early 1980s, from the age of 13, Will spent his spare time as a rap DJ at parties. He rapped between records. He was influenced by the style of a hip-hop band called Grandmaster Flash and the Furious Five.

Here is Will (right) and Jeff in the 1980s. Some rappers thought their music was too "soft".

DJ Jazzy Jeff

In 1984, at the age of 16, Will went to a party where the well-known DJ, Jazzy Jeff, was playing. Will asked if he could rap with him. He agreed and they quickly became friends. They started to perform together at parties and called themselves DJ Jazzy Jeff and the Fresh Prince.

Rock the House

The duo sent tapes of their music to a record **producer** in Philadelphia. He passed them on to a local record company. The company made their first single, "Girls Ain't Nothing But Trouble". The record was played in lots of clubs in Philadelphia.

A year before Will left school, a much bigger company called Jive Records heard their record. They paid Will and Jeff $15,000 (£9,800) each for the rights to sell it. Very soon, it was a hit in the United States and the UK – 100,000 copies were sold.

In 1987, just two weeks before Will left high school, their first **album** was released. It was called *Rock the House* and 600,000 copies sold quickly. Will and Jeff went on tour and were amazed to be met by crowds of fans. They were famous!

Not serious enough?

The duo's music was about young people's worries, and the fun they had. Often, it was funny. Other rappers did not like their music. They thought it was not serious enough. They preferred rap music that was about gangs and street-life. They thought rap music should talk angrily about the problems faced by African-Americans.

Hip-hop bands like Public Enemy have hard-hitting, political lyrics. Will and Jeff's lyrics were more fun.

Even though some rap fans did not like their music, Will and Jeff had huge success. In 1989 they won the first-ever **Grammy** for a rap record. The song was called "Parents Just Don't Understand".

Here today, gone tomorrow

By the time Will was 18 he had $2 million (£1.3 million) and 8 cars. By the time he was 21, he had nothing left! He had spent too much on having a good time. Also, he had a big **tax** bill to pay.

In 1990, with a debt to pay, and record sales falling, Will decided to try a new career. He wanted to be an actor, so he moved to Los Angeles.

Summertime

In 1991 Will worked with Jeff on their final album, *Homebase*. The single "Summertime" won them a second Grammy. DJ Jazzy Jeff and Fresh Prince made music together until 1993. In 1997 Will recorded an album of his own called *Big Willie Style*.

Here's Will at a music award evening, with famous pop singer Celine Dion.

Rap rhythms

Listen to a variety of rap beats and try to clap them out at the same time. A rhythm is made of strong beats and weak beats. Here is an example (the strong beats are in *italic*):

Jack and *Jill* went *up* the *hill*.

Now have a go at writing your own rap lyrics.

Steps to follow:

1. Pick a subject you like a lot, such as new shoes or a holiday.

2. The lines in a rap usually rhyme (for example, "shoes" rhymes with "news"). Jot down some words to do with your subject that rhyme.

3. Write a good first line that has a strong beat. Clap out the beat.

4. Write a second line with a similar beat. Try to make the last word of the first and second line rhyme.

5. Keep going until you've finished four to six lines. Each pair of lines could have a different rhyme.

Clap out the beat to some of Will Smith's music, such as Will and Jeff's "Parents Just Don't Understand".

Here's an example:

I *went* to the *shops* and I've *got* some *news*

I *bought* a *pair* of *cool* new *shoes*.

The Fresh Prince of Bel-Air

In 1990 Will went to Los Angeles because it is the movie-making centre of the United States. He hoped that his fame would help him get an acting job.

A lucky meeting

Will had a lucky meeting with a record **producer**, Benny Medina. Benny had an idea for a television comedy series. He thought that Will would be good in it. Benny managed to persuade a television company to make the series. He also got Will an **audition** for a star part. The audition went well. Will got the part. His acting career had begun!

In *The Fresh Prince of Bel-Air*, Will's character often clashes with his rich cousin, Carlton (left).

A family sitcom

The television series was called *The Fresh Prince of Bel-Air*. It was a **sitcom**, which meant that it was about funny events in a realistic setting. Will played the part of a confident, rather wild youngster from Philadelphia. The humour comes from the fact that he goes to live with wealthy relatives in one of the richest parts of Los Angeles, called Bel-Air. The rich family try to make him behave better. Will's character has other ideas and often upsets them.

At first, Will made lots of mistakes as an actor. He spoke too quietly, forgot his lines, and looked into the camera. He had never acted before. However, Will was determined to learn. He studied the **professionals** he was working with and improved every day.

TV hit

The Fresh Prince of Bel-Air won awards and Will was voted favourite television actor in 1991. The series ran for six years. Will made sure Jeff had a part as his best friend.

Big screen

In 1992 Will got a small part in a film called *Where the Day Takes You*. His second role was in a comedy film called *Made in America*. The famous actress Whoopi Goldberg taught him that he must be more sensible. Filmmakers have no time for actors who mess around between scenes. Will played a similar character in *Made in America* to the one in *The Fresh Prince of Bel-Air*. He worried that he would always be given the same kind of role. His aim was to get a more serious part in a bigger movie.

Whoopi Goldberg and Will Smith acting in the film *Made in America*.

Rapping live

Prepare your own **rap** performance. Your rap lyrics can be:

- lyrics you have written yourself (see page 15)
- Will Smith's lyrics (ask a parent to help you find some on the Internet)
- a nursery **rhyme** with a strong beat (for example, "Hey diddle diddle").

Steps to follow:

1. Get used to the beat. Experiment to find which words, or parts of words, the strong and weak beats fall on. Clapping as you say the words will help. Use a pencil to mark the strong beats.

2. Experiment with the sounds of the words. You could stretch out some words and break up or shorten others. You could also repeat parts of words. For example, "Hey diddle, diddle" could become "Heeey, did- did- diddle".

3. Rap artists move to the beat, too. Relax and try to let your whole body get into the beat as you say the words.

4. Ask a friend to play the beat on a percussion instrument, or clap it out.

5. When you are happy with your rap, perform it in front of an audience.

Interact with your audience. Look at them, and encourage them to clap to the beat.

In the movies

Will Smith was delighted when he was given the leading role in a **drama** called *Six Degrees of Separation* in 1993. Dramas have a serious theme. Will played a character who tricks his way into the home of a wealthy family. It was a difficult role to perform. Will took acting lessons and worked hard. Will said of his work for *Six Degrees of Separation*: "My drive was the fact that … they didn't think that I could do it."

A smooth move into the movies

Will's hard work paid off. Film critics praised his acting skills in the movie. It was the beginning of Will's movie success. From then on, he was offered major roles in all kinds of films.

Will plays a trickster in the drama *Six Degrees of Separation*.

Real-life drama

Six Degrees of Separation was based on a true story. Will later starred in another real-life movie that was a box-office hit. *Ali* (2001) was a **biography** of the boxing champion, Muhammad Ali. Will had to copy the way Ali spoke, moved, and boxed! To look like the boxer, he had to build up his muscles in the gym.

Career first?

Will felt he had failed when he and Sheree divorced in 1995. Many people thought Will had put his career first and not spent enough time with his family. When he married again in 1997, he didn't make the same mistake. His new wife was actress Jada Pinkett. In 1998 they had a son, Jaden, and in 2000 they had a daughter, Willow.

To look like the boxer in *Ali*, Will had to build up his muscles and weight by 16 kilograms (35 pounds).

Action

Will played an action hero for the first time in a movie called *Bad Boys* (1995). He played a wild cop and worked alongside **co-star** Martin Lawrence. Lawrence was a comedian as well as an actor. The cops and robbers action involved lots of running around and shooting. *Bad Boys* was a hit.

Sci-fi

Will's next challenge was a **sci-fi** action film called *Independence Day* (1996). He played the part of a fighter pilot who had to stop aliens from invading Earth.

It was a box office hit and soon brought in $800 million (£515 million)!

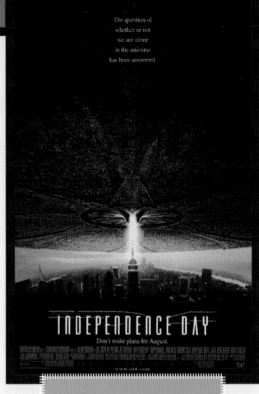

This poster is advertising *Independence Day*. After seeing the movie, people often stopped Will in the street to congratulate him.

Film genres

Films are described by their **genre** (the type of film they are):
- Comedy: light-hearted plots; funny things are said, and happen
- Drama: serious plots, often about realistic people and situations
- Sci-fi (or science fiction): usually set in outer space and/or the future
- Action: action films are full of exciting events, such as fights, car chases, and explosions.

Movies can be a mix of genres. For example, *Independence Day* is a sci-fi action movie.

Comedy

There is often a comic element in Will's movies. *Men in Black* (1997) was a sci-fi comedy action film. The movie was so successful that Will took the same role in *Men in Black II*, in 2002.

A famous film **producer**, Steven Spielberg, rang Will to ask him to be in *Men in Black*. Will said "yes", but he was a bit worried about doing another movie about aliens after *Independence Day*. This scene is from *Men in Black II*.

Will starred with his son, Jaden, in *The Pursuit of Happyness*, in 2006.

The amount of money Will earned as an actor rocketed. For his part in *Where the Day Takes You* (1992), he earned US$50,000 (£32,000). For his part in *Men in Black II* (2002), he earned US$20 million (£13 million)!

Awards and nominations

An **Oscar** is a major movie award in the United States. Will received two Oscar **nominations** for his parts in the movies, *Ali* and *The Pursuit of Happyness*.

Overbrook Entertainment

Around 1997–99, Will started up his own company called Overbrook Entertainment. The company makes films and television programmes. It has produced hits starring Will, such as *The Pursuit of Happyness*. The company also manages artists and helps unknown music performers record music.

Oops!

Will has made a few mistakes. One was to turn down a lead part in *The Matrix*. Actor Keanu Reeves took the part instead. The movie was a massive hit.

Film poster

Imagine that Will Smith is to star in a new movie. It is your job to decide its title and what the movie will be about. Finally, you have to design a poster to persuade people to go and see it!

Steps to follow:

1. What sort of movie would suit Will Smith? Pick a genre from the box on page 22.

2. What part would Will play? Describe the plot in a sentence. For example: "Will plays a cop who has to track down criminals who have stolen a deadly poison."

3. Think of an exciting title. A short title (such as *Wild Man Cop*) is more likely to grab people's attention than a longer title.

4. Sketch out your poster. Think about answers to these questions:

- How big should the movie title be?

- What kind of picture would be exciting? (A comedy movie would need a different kind of image to an action movie.)

- What colours best reflect the mood and plot? Try different materials (pens, paints, pastels).

5. Finish your poster. Ask your friends if they would go to see this movie.

Don't clutter your poster with too much information. A simple, dramatic design is often the most eye-catching.

Multi-talented

By working hard Will managed to achieve a movie star career. But he stayed a musician, too. He performed the theme songs for many of his movies, such as *Men in Black*. Between 1997 and 2005 he brought out four solo **albums** and a *Greatest Hits* album.

African-American actor

As an African-American actor Will has led the way for other African-Americans in Hollywood. *Bad Boys* (1995) was one of the first-ever action movies to star two leading African-American actors. In 2008 he set the record for starring in the most consecutive (one after another) movies that each made US$100 million (£65 million) at the box office. Over his acting life, he's received about 30 awards and about 50 **nominations**.

Will's fans live all around the world. Here, Will is signing autographs in New York, USA.

Always busy

Will is always picking up new skills. He has become a film **producer** as well an as actor, in films such as *Hancock* and *Seven Pounds*. In 2008 he started to work on a role in his first epic movie *The Last Pharaoh*.

His long list of wide-ranging skills includes fluently speaking Spanish and playing chess well.

Family man

Although Will made a mistake with his first marriage by giving too much time to his career, he now puts his family first. Because he and his wife are both actors, together they are aware of the dangers of a Hollywood lifestyle. They protect their privacy and relationship. They live with their children in Los Angeles in a large home where Will has his own recording studio.

This shows Will with his daughter, Willow, and son Jaden.

Timeline

1968   Will is born in Philadelphia, Pennsylvania, USA on 25 September.

1989   The Fresh Prince and **DJ** Jazzy Jeff win their first major music award (a **Grammy**).

1990   Will takes a role in the new TV **sitcom**, *The Fresh Prince of Bel-Air*.

1991   The Fresh Prince and Jazzy Jeff win a second Grammy for "Summertime".

Will Smith became a multimillionaire while he was still a teenager.

1992   Will marries Sheree Zampino; their son, Trey, is born.

1993   The Fresh Prince and DJ Jazzy Jeff release their last **album**, *Code Red*. Will appears in his first serious film role, in *Six Degrees of Separation*.

1995   Will stars as a hero in *Bad Boys*. Sheree and Will divorce.

1996   Will stars in *Independence Day*.

1997	Will releases the solo album *Big Willie Style*. He marries Jada Pinkett. He stars in *Men in Black*.
1998	Will and Jada's son, Jaden, is born.
1999	Will stars in comedy action movie, *Wild Wild West*.
2000	Daughter, Willow, is born.
2003	Will and Jada produce and create a sitcom called *All of Us*.
2004	Will produces and stars in the **sci-fi** movie, *I, Robot*. He also stars in *Shark Tale*.
2005	Will produces and stars in the romantic comedy, *Hitch*.
2007	Will receives a **nomination** for an **Oscar**, for his part in *The Pursuit of Happyness*. He also stars in *I am Legend*. His year's earnings are estimated at US$31 million (£20 million).
2008	Will Smith works as a **producer** on five films.

Will Smith starred in the children's movie *Shark Tale* – he spoke the words of a little fish called Oscar.

Glossary

album record with several songs or pieces of music on it. Will has made four solo albums.

audition test that a singer or actor does to show if they are good enough for a particular part in a film or television programme. Will passed his audition for *Six Degrees of Separation*, and got the part he wanted.

biography story of a real person's life. *Ali* was a movie biography of a real boxer's life.

co-star actor who plays alongside another star in a movie. Will co-starred with actress Charlize Theron in *Hancock*.

disco music type of music played for people to dance to. Clubs where disco music is played are sometimes called discos.

DJ (short for disc jockey) person who plays music, such as records. Rap DJs talk over the records they are playing. A rap DJ might also play the backing while another artist (called an MC, or Master of Ceremonies) raps.

drama exciting and serious story. A drama movie is a movie with a serious story and realistic setting and characters.

genre type of something. Film genres range from spaghetti Westerns to biographical dramas.

Grammy award for special achievements in record-making. The actual Grammy is a small copy of an old style record-player (called a gramophone).

hip-hop culture that includes fashion and a type of music. Hip-hop music uses rap.

inspiration something or someone who spurs you on to achieve something similar. Will Smith might be an inspiration to actors who are just starting out in their career.

nomination when someone has been suggested by others to win an award. Several names are put forward for movie awards, such as the Oscars.

Oscar in the movie world, an award given for achievements in film-making. The actual Oscar award is a gold statue.

producer someone who helps to make a film or record. Producers are usually in charge of money in film- and record-making.

professional person that does a job for money. Professional people often have lots of knowledge to share about the job they do.

rap type of poetry that is spoken out loud. A musical beat is often played while the rap artist raps.

rhyme words that sound the same. "Hat" and "bat" rhyme.

rhythm regular or repeated beat in a poem, rap lyric, or piece of music

sci-fi (short for science-fiction) any story that is to do with the future or outer space. Sci-fi movies are often set in the future, or involve space ships and aliens.

single in the world of music, one song that is sold on its own. A single is often brought out to help sell an album.

sitcom series of television programmes that are funny and set in a realistic setting, such as a home or office. A good sitcom makes people laugh.

tax money that people have to pay to the government. The amount of tax you have to pay depends on how much money you earn.

Find out more

Books

A History of Hip-Hop: The Roots of Rap, Thomas Hatch (Red Bricklearning, 2005)

Culture in Action: Hip-Hop, Jim Mack (Raintree, 2009)

Outkast (Hip-hop part 2), Jacquelyn Simone (Mason Crest Publishers, 2008)

People in the News: Will Smith, Michael V. Uschan (Lucent Books, 2009)

Star Files: Will Smith, Mark Stewart (Raintree, 2005)

Websites

www.fanpop.com/spots/will-smith
Fans of Will have created this website. It has lots of fun images and videos of Will.

www.museumwales.ac.uk
Listen to some rap written by young people. Search for "rap" to find the link.

www.willsmith.com
This is Will's own website. It contains information about all of Will's albums, films, and other news.

Index